First published in paperback in 2009
by Evans Brothers Limited
2A Portman Mansions
Chiltern Street
London W1U 6NR

Printed in China

© Evans Brothers Limited 2004

British Library Cataloguing in Publication data.

Powell, Jillian
Food allergies. - (Like Me, Like You)
1. Food allergies - Juvenile literature
I. Title
618.9'2975

ISBN 9780237538583

Acknowledgements

The author and publishers would like to thank the following for their help with this book:

Aneil, Santosh and Sanjay Mehta, Aunt Kally, Joshua Young, Kieran, Ricky and Haresh and the rest of the Mehta family.

Thanks also to the Anaphylaxis Campaign for their help in the preparation of this book.

All photographs by Gareth Boden

Credits

Series Editor: Louise John
Editor: Julia Bird
Designer: Mark Holt
Production: Jenny Mulvanny

The **Anaphylaxis** campaign
Helping people with severe allergies live their lives

LIKE ME LIKE YOU

Aneil has a
FOOD ALLERGY

Evans

LIKE ME LIKE YOU

Aneil has a FOOD ALLERGY

JILLIAN POWELL

Evans

Hi, my name is Aneil.
I live at home with
Mum and Dad and
my brother Sanjay.
I like swimming,
riding my bike
and playing
cricket and
table tennis.

I have a **food allergy**. If I eat anything containing nuts, they make me ill. Just touching nuts can start my allergy. If Sanjay eats them, he has to wash his hands before coming near me!

FOOD ALLERGY

A **food allergy** is when the body reacts badly to food that is harmless for most people.

7

My family found out I had a food allergy when I was three years old. I ate some nuts and they made me cough. My lips and eyes puffed up and I was sick. They had to take me to hospital to have an **injection** of **adrenaline** to make me better.

Now I have to be very careful not to eat any foods that contain nuts. Breakfast cereals sometimes contain nuts, so Mum and I have to check the labels to make sure I can eat them.

Most food allergies begin in childhood. Some children grow out of allergies, especially to milk or eggs.

Today, we're going to my cousin Kieran's birthday party. Mum is making hot dogs for the party so we need to buy some bread rolls. Mum asks the baker if there are any nuts or traces of nuts – which means tiny bits of nuts – in the rolls.

If I eat nuts accidentally and get ill, Mum has to inject me with adrenaline from a special pen. Mum always carries the pens and I keep two pens at school as well. Mum injects my leg like this, but I have to sit or lie down.

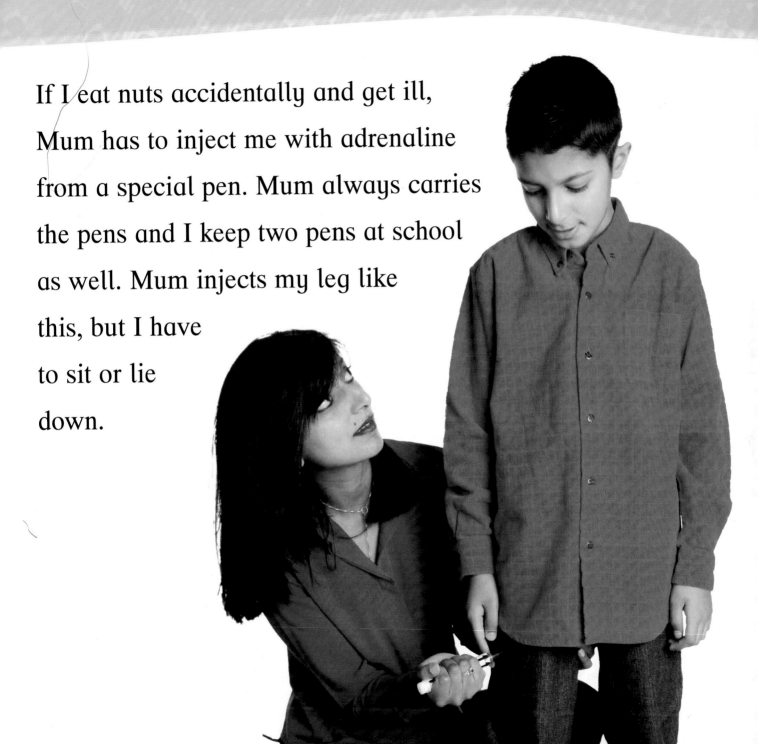

Shopping can take a long time, because Mum and I have to check all the food labels. We check to see that there are no nuts or traces of nuts in anything we're buying.

Cakes, biscuits and chocolate can all contain nuts. Lots of other foods can contain traces of nuts. Even foods like ice cream and pasta sauce can contain tiny bits of nuts that could make me ill.

We arrive at Kieran's house early. Mum has brought the hot dogs. She needs to check with Aunty Kally if there is any food at the party that I won't be able to eat because it contains nuts.

I say hello to my cousins Kieran, Haresh and Ricky and their dog Rex. I would love to have a dog too, but we can't because animal fur can give me a reaction called **eczema** that makes my skin itch.

OTHER ALLERGIES

Children with food allergies often have other conditions such as **asthma** and **eczema**.

I love quad bikes and we always have a great time playing on them at Kieran's house. Rex wants to join in too!

Mum and Aunty Kally are checking the food in the kitchen. They read all the labels to make sure nothing contains nuts or traces of nuts. They have to check everything, like the bread for the burgers, biscuits, and cakes.

I have a big family! My granddad and grandma are at the party, as well as my mum and dad, aunt and uncle and cousins. There is lots of food for us to eat.

There are some special Asian dishes like **lentil** curry and ludu, which are sweets made from flour, sugar and milk. Mum reminds me that these dishes might have nuts in them.

I'm sitting next to my friend Joshua. We're in the same class at school. Joshua has food allergies too. He can't eat the lentil curry because he's allergic to lentils.

The foods that most often cause allergies include milk, eggs, nuts, wheat, fish, shell fish and soy beans.

Joshua has brought a big birthday present to the party for Kieran. Kieran loves getting presents!

It's time for Kieran to cut the cake! He blows out the candles first. It's a sponge cake. Mum has checked that it has no nuts in it, so it's okay for me to eat.

Aunty Kally is giving me, Joshua and Sanjay party bags to take home. They have little toys and sweets in them. I can't wait to look in mine!

It's been a great party but it's time to go home now. We say goodbye to Aunty Kally and to our cousins.

When we get home, Sanjay and I look in our party bags. I got a chocolate bar that might have nuts in it, so Mum tells me to swop with Sanjay. His chocolate bar is safe for me to eat.

The worst thing about having a food allergy is that you can't always eat what everyone else is eating. Sometimes I have to miss a party if we don't know what the food will be like. Mum or Dad stay at home with me.

But there are lots of foods I enjoy that are safe for me to eat. One of my favourites is homemade pizza!

Glossary

Adrenaline a medicine which helps to calm allergic reactions, making it easier to breathe

Asthma a condition that causes problems with breathing. It can be an allergy

Eczema a condition that causes a rash and itching. It can be an allergy

Food allergy when the body reacts badly to food that is harmless for most people

Injection having a prick from a needle to put something into our body

Lentil a kind of plant seed which is eaten as a vegetable

Index

Further Information

UNITED KINGDOM
The Anaphylaxis Campaign
Tel. 01252 542029
www.anaphylaxis.org.uk
Information and guidance for people with the severe food allergy called anaphylaxis. A range of educational products, including information sheets and videos are available.

Allergy UK
Tel: 020 8303 8525
www.allergyuk.org
Up-to-date information, advice and support for people with allergies. Information fact sheets are available.

UNITED STATES OF AMERICA
The Food Allergy and Anaphylaxis Network
Resources and support for allergy sufferers, as well as tips on how to manage food allergies.
www.foodallergy.org

AUSTRALIA
Anaphylaxis Australia
Tel: 1300 728 000
www.allergyfacts.org.au
Practical help for food allergy sufferers.

NEW ZEALAND
Allergy New Zealand Inc
Tel: 09 623 3912
www.allergy.org.nz
Education and information for allergy sufferers.

BOOKS
Allergies (Feeling Ill?), Jillian Powell, Evans 2007

Food Allergy (Explaining), Carol Ballard, Franklin Watts 2008

Let's Talk about Having Allergies, Elisabeth Weitzman, Powerkids Press 2003

Why Do My Eyes Itch? And Other Questions About Allergies (Body Matters)
Angela Royston, Heinemann Library 2003